Spotlight on Social Justice

THE FIGHT OVER CHOICE

THE HISTORY AND FUTURE OF REPRODUCTIVE RIGHTS

LAUREN KUKLA

TWENTY-FIRST CENTURY BOOKS / MINNEAPOLIS

Content Warning

This book contains material that may be triggering for some readers, including brief discussions of rape and suicide. If you or someone you know is in need of support, please reach out to the following resources:

- **National Suicide Prevention Lifeline**
  Available 24/7: 1-800-273-TALK (1-800-273-8255)
  Chat: suicidepreventionlifeline.org/chat
- **The Trevor Project (for LGBTQ+ Youth)**
  Available 24/7: 1-866-488-7386
  Text START to 678-678
  Chat: thetrevorproject.org/help

To the amazing team of doctors, nurses, and midwives who saw me through my third pregnancy while writing this book.

Twenty-First Century Books™
An imprint of Lerner Publishing Group, Inc.
241 First Avenue North
Minneapolis, MN 55401 USA

For reading levels and more information, look up this title at www.lernerbooks.com.

Main body text set in Bembo Std Regular
Typeface provided by Monotype Typography.

Library of Congress Cataloging-in-Publication Data

Names: Kukla, Lauren, author.
Title: The fight over choice : the history and future of reproductive rights / by Lauren Kukla.
Description: Minneapolis : Twenty-First Century Books, [2026] | Series: Spotlight on social justice | Includes bibliographical references and index. | Audience: Ages 11–18 | Audience: Grades 7–9 | Summary: "People across time, especially women, have faced barriers to reproductive health access. But what all does reproductive health cover? And why are people working to protect and improve it? Learn about the history and future of reproductive justice"—Provided by publisher.
Identifiers: LCCN 2024043972 (print) | LCCN 2024043973 (ebook) | ISBN 9798765644140 (library binding) | ISBN 9798765684948 (paperback) | ISBN 9798765683071 (epub)
Subjects: LCSH: Reproductive rights—Juvenile literature. | Reproductive rights—History—Juvenile literature. | Reproductive health—Juvenile literature.
Classification: LCC HQ766 .K88 2026 (print) | LCC HQ766 (ebook) | DDC 306.4/61—dc23/eng/20241226

LC record available at https://lccn.loc.gov/2024043972
LC ebook record available at https://lccn.loc.gov/2024043973

Manufactured in the United States of America
1 – CG – 7/15/25

CONTENTS

INTRODUCTION

Every human being is here because of human reproduction. People may experience reproductive health in different ways, but it is an essential part of the human experience.

Reproductive health relates to the organs and biological processes that affect reproductive organs during all stages of life. But it is much more than these physical parts working as they should. Reproductive health encompasses a person's overall well-being. This includes experiencing safe and consensual sexual activity, accessing accurate information about reproductive health, having safe and effective health care, and feeling empowered to make health decisions. Such decisions might include whether to have children and when, how to express gender identity, and when and how to engage in sexual activity.

Understanding Sex and Gender

Many people use the words *gender* and *sex* interchangeably to describe a person's gender identity. But most scientists and physicians now view gender as a social construct. This means

In 2023 the US birth rate was 11 births per 1,000 people, while Canada's was 10.2, and Mexico's was 16.3.

people often associate certain behaviors, appearances, and other outward expressions with a specific gender. But just because someone expresses those associated traits does not mean they identify with that gender. Instead, someone's gender identity is their innate sense of their own gender.

Sex refers to a set of physical characteristics that define a person as biologically male or female. These characteristics include anatomy, hormone levels, and gene expression. Everyone is assigned a sex at birth. And people also often correlate someone's assigned sex at birth with their gender, such as female with woman and male with man. Someone who identifies as the gender corresponding with their sex assigned at birth is cisgender. But someone's assigned sex may or may not match their gender. Transgender people have a gender identity that does not align with their assigned sex. Other people are nonbinary. This means they don't identify strictly with either binary gender. Both sex and gender can shift and change over time. People can alter physical sex characteristics, such as anatomy and hormone levels, to better match their gender identity.

In this book, we'll discuss issues related to anatomy, gender, and sex. This also includes the many reproductive justice issues facing transgender, nonbinary, and other gender-diverse people, particularly in gaining safe and equitable health care. We'll use gender-neutral language whenever possible. However, only people assigned female at birth can physically bear children. While this group can include some men, nonbinary people, and people of other genders, women have historically faced the most reproductive rights issues and injustice surrounding menstruation, pregnancy, and birth. So, for simplicity, we'll use the terms *woman* and *female* to discuss this group in this context. When discussing anatomy, we'll use *male* to describe a person assigned male at birth and *female* to describe a person assigned female at birth.

Reproductive Justice

Reproductive health is a human right. However, people, particularly women, have faced extreme barriers to quality reproductive health care throughout history. This book will explore some of these barriers and how people and human rights organizations have fought to overcome them through reproductive justice. Reproductive justice is achieved when the right to reproductive health is protected, giving everyone the social, political, and economic power to make fully informed decisions about their bodies and general well-being.

Political leaders often talk about reproductive justice in the context of divisive issues including contraception, abortion, and gender identity and expression. However, reproductive justice covers so much more than these hot-button topics. It includes people having access to accurate information about their bodies so they can make informed decisions about their health and accessing safe and effective health care from a provider who

Reproductive Rights for Intersex People

Not all people are born strictly biologically male or female. Experts estimate that 2 percent of humans are born intersex. This means their internal or external anatomy does not align with the binary definitions of male and female. For instance, an intersex baby born with female reproductive organs and chromosomes may also have male genitalia. There is a wide range of intersex expressions. Many intersex babies undergo irreversible surgical procedures to align their physical characteristics with a single gender. Doctors perform these procedures before the baby is old enough to consent to them. These procedures can cause infertility, pain, and other issues. As these children grow, they often face gender dysphoria and discrimination. Advocates for intersex rights believe intersex individuals should have the right to decide about having surgery when they're old enough to understand and consent. This means moving away from surgeries on babies and focusing on letting people make their own choices later.

In 2024 the United Nations Human Rights Council examined harmful laws and practices affecting intersex people. It aims to protect their reproductive rights and bodily autonomy.

empowers them to do so. It includes the right to have children if a person chooses to. And it includes the right to engage in safe, consensual sexual activity with a partner of choice.

CHAPTER ONE

Midwives and Wandering Wombs

While all people have struggled to find reproductive justice throughout history, the issue overwhelmingly affects women. This is largely because most societies viewed women as inferior to men for centuries. As a result, most medical researchers and practitioners were men until the late 1900s. Long-standing myths about women and their bodies fed into biases, including the false beliefs that women were more emotional than men and more likely to exaggerate a medical condition to seek attention. These biases paired with a general lack of understanding about the female body led to inadequate reproductive health care for centuries. But humans have been around for far longer than practicing physicians, and for most of humanity's history, women's health care was the responsibility of other women.

Midwives and Healers

Since humanity's earliest days, experienced female healers and midwives provided reproductive health care to women. These practitioners held knowledge of folk medicine and natural remedies. They used herbs and ancient techniques to aid in menstrual issues, contraception, abortion, and pain relief. Female healers helped birth babies with the support of female friends and relatives. In some cultures, men were banned from viewing or participating in the birth process. Starting around 3500 BCE midwifery was a paid profession throughout Egypt and the Mediterranean. Egyptian writings dating back more than 3,500 years discuss birthing techniques and best practices for midwives. During this time, midwives held an important place in society.

Three midwives tend to a pregnant person sitting in a birthing chair in the 1500s. During the Middle Ages (500–1500) it was common practice for people to give birth in an upright position, often in a birthing chair.

The Rise of Medicine

Starting around 300 BCE Greek thinkers, beginning with Hippocrates, formalized medicine into a scientific field with trained physicians. Before this time, superstition ruled much of Greek medicine, with many people believing gods and goddesses caused diseases and illnesses. Hippocrates separated medicine from religion. As a teacher, he created an organized establishment of trained physicians who used scientific principles to care for patients. However, these physicians were mostly male, and unlike midwives, they had a limited understanding of female bodies.

The scientific fields of biology and anatomy were still young. As a result, these physicians held beliefs about women's bodies that seem outlandish today. Hippocrates argued that menstruation caused diseases in women. The cure was pregnancy. This aligned with social views that a woman's role was to bear and care for children. Ancient Greek physicians believed women's bodies were too wet because of menstrual blood, leading to an imbalance in the body. Uteruses were thought to cause "mischief" if women weren't pregnant. The physicians accused uteruses of "wandering throughout the body" causing disease. These physicians were also likely to blame any complications with fertility, pregnancy, or birth on the woman experiencing them. The ancient Greek philosopher Aristotle went so far as to describe the female body as a male body "turn'd outside in."

A New Handbook

In the 100s CE Greek physician Soranus wrote *On Midwifery and the Diseases of Women*. Little is known about how he obtained the information for this book, but it covered contraception, birth, abortion, and other reproductive topics. It dispelled many of the more outlandish Greek beliefs about women and became a guidebook for practicing midwives for the next 1,500 years.

The Middle Ages were challenging for women across Europe. The rise of Christianity fueled negative beliefs about women and their bodies. According to the church, women were inherently weak, deceitful, and prone to sin. By the 1300s it was illegal for women to practice medicine in Europe. Around this time, a book called *De secretus mulierium*, or *The Secrets of Women*, became a popular resource for male church leaders in structuring laws and beliefs surrounding

Indigenous Practices

Among the Navajo people, female healers play an essential role in women's reproductive health. They use traditional herbs to support pregnancy, childbirth, and overall wellness.

Indigenous people in North America had well-established practices and traditions surrounding reproductive health care. Practices varied across different nations, but most relied on trained midwives and healers to provide reproductive care to the women in their community. These providers had deep knowledge of their region's plants, herbs, and folk remedies. These remedies aided women in abortions, contraception, menstrual issues, and other reproductive health concerns. Indigenous communities also often held more fluid views on gender than their European counterparts. Many nations viewed gender and sex as separate constructs. They recognized many more genders that did not align with the gender binary of man and woman. Historically, individuals who didn't identify as a man or a woman were usually treated equally to those who did. They could take on positions of importance within their social group.

women's bodies. The book reinforced the idea that miscarriage, pregnancy, and birth complications were the woman's fault.

Across the Sea

In the late 1400s European explorers traveled to the Caribbean, North America, and South America, calling them the New World. However, millions of Indigenous peoples already inhabited this area. Europeans regarded the Indigenous peoples as inferior and did not respect their claim to the land. By the mid-1600s Europeans had established colonies throughout North, South, and Central America. They murdered, enslaved, or forcibly relocated Indigenous peoples living in colonized areas.

Without a formal medical system, midwifery became essential to medical care in colonial North America. By the 1700s many midwives were paid for their work. Access to reproductive health care varied by colony, depending on the reproductive beliefs of the colonists' home countries. In the British colonies, white colonial women had access to abortion and contraception with no legal barriers. At the time, most British people believed that life began at quickening, or the point at which a pregnant person feels the fetus move. This usually happens at about twenty weeks of pregnancy. Abortions were common in the British colonies before quickening. In French colonies, abortion was illegal, but it was openly and frequently performed with few legal consequences. In Spanish and Portuguese colonies, abortions were illegal and performed in secret.

REFLECT

In many ways, women living in colonial North America had greater reproductive freedom than women living in modern North America. Why is it important to understand the history of reproductive rights when discussing the future of reproductive justice?

CHAPTER TWO
The Tide Turns

The US declared its independence from Great Britain in 1776. Canada followed in 1867, and Mexico had gained independence from Spain in 1821. These new nations created laws governing their people, including their reproductive health. Many of these laws chipped away at the reproductive freedoms many colonial women had access to.

By the mid-1800s medicine was advancing. Scientists and physicians developed the first vaccines, discovered the importance of hygiene in disease prevention, and started using anesthetics during surgeries. During this time, male physicians were also increasingly involved in women's health care. However, social norms at the time limited the physicians' ability to study women's bodies. Women and doctors alike limited physical exams and avoided discussing sensitive topics related to women's health with one another.

The AMA

In 1847 US physicians founded the American Medical Association (AMA). The organization aimed to improve public health by standardizing medical care across the US.

However, all the early AMA physicians were male. To standardize medicine, the AMA worked to phase out female practitioners, including people who provided reproductive health services, such as midwives. At the time, most people in Western societies still viewed a woman's primary role as to bear and care for children. Christianity, which was the most common religion in the US at the time, supported this view.

"In sorrow, thou shalt bring forth children, and thy desire shall be to thy husband, and he shall rule over thee."

—Genesis 3:16, Twenty-First Century King James Bible

Abortion and contraception also conflicted with Christian beliefs about life. The AMA took a firm stance against abortion, arguing that it was not only immoral but medically dangerous. And the organization didn't consider contraception to be part of a physician's medical practice.

The Father of Gynecology

In the 1840s Dr. J. Marion Sims became one of the first male physicians to focus on women's medicine. He developed equipment, techniques, and surgical procedures that revolutionized gynecology. But he also performed painful experiments on enslaved and low-income immigrant women without their consent. Even after the invention of anesthesia, Sims refused to provide pain relief for these women.

In 1855 Sims founded the first women's hospital in New York City. He became the head of the AMA in 1876. Sims improved the lives of many women. However, his views on a woman's lack of bodily autonomy, including his belief in a physician's right to run tests on and treat a female patient as they see fit, with or without her consent, continue to influence the field.

Pain Management

Into the early 1900s many North American women gave birth at home under the care of relatives and midwives without medical intervention. Physicians rarely offered pain management to women who delivered under their care, even when women asked for it. Some physicians thought anesthesia could harm the baby. And most people at the time viewed pain as a natural part of childbirth. Many doctors also doubted women's complaints of pain. Doctors felt they were the best judges of whether a woman's pain was severe enough to warrant anesthesia. This view influenced medical beliefs into modern times. Women, especially women of color, still fight to have their pain taken seriously.

Restricting Choice

While advances in medicine and the field of gynecology were changing the way physicians viewed women's health care, lawmakers began taking steps to limit women's bodily autonomy by creating new laws affecting contraception and abortion. Although contraception options were limited, women had been using acidic solutions and spermicides to limit unwanted pregnancies for decades. That all changed in the late 1860s when New York salesman Anthony Comstock, a devout Christian, launched a campaign against contraception.

By 1873 Comstock had successfully lobbied Congress to pass a law banning the distribution of "obscene literature and articles of immoral use." Under the law,

REFLECT

What are some arguments for and against restricting personal choices related to reproductive health? How do these restrictions affect people's lives?

contraception and abortion-related products were considered obscene and immoral. Sending them across state lines was a federal crime. Meanwhile, individual states were also restricting abortion and contraception access. In the wake of the new Comstock Act, twenty-four states passed laws banning the distribution of contraception. In Connecticut, the use of birth control became a crime, even among married couples. Abortion faced similar restrictions. By 1910 abortion at any stage of pregnancy was outlawed in every US state.

Reproductive Justice for Enslaved Women

Black women in the southern US faced a very different landscape for their reproductive health in the 1800s than white women. Since 1619 when the first enslaved people arrived in the colonies, many white people saw Black people as property. As enslavement spread across the southern US, many Black people lost all reproductive freedom. White owners forced enslaved people to bear children, often resulting from rape. They also made enslaved people breastfeed and care for the owner's children. Enslavers could forcibly take away and sell Black women's children at any moment. Health care aimed to keep enslaved people productive, but providers often administered it without the enslaved person's consent. Many white people believed Black people did not experience pain in the same way as white people, so enslaved Black women were subjected to experimental surgeries with no pain relief. Even after enslavement ended in 1865, people continued to perform medical experiments on Black women. This history of injustice led to the health-care disparities that Black people, especially women, still face.

King Condom

By the early 1900s condoms were the primary form of contraception. Although condoms had existed for centuries, the introduction of materials such as latex in the 1920s made them easier to use and more effective. Earlier versions of condoms were made from animal intestines or rubber. Condoms were much better at preventing pregnancy than the spermicides and folk remedies women had been using. They also prevented sexually transmitted infections (STIs).

But condoms had a downside. Only men could wear them, so women had to rely on their partners for contraception. Additionally, condoms required prescriptions in some states, and doctors only prescribed them for the prevention of diseases. Using condoms as contraception was against the law in some states, even for married couples. However, views on contraception were starting to change again. In 1912 a new movement emerged to increase women's knowledge of their contraception options, shift society's views on sexual activity, and end the legal restrictions surrounding contraception.

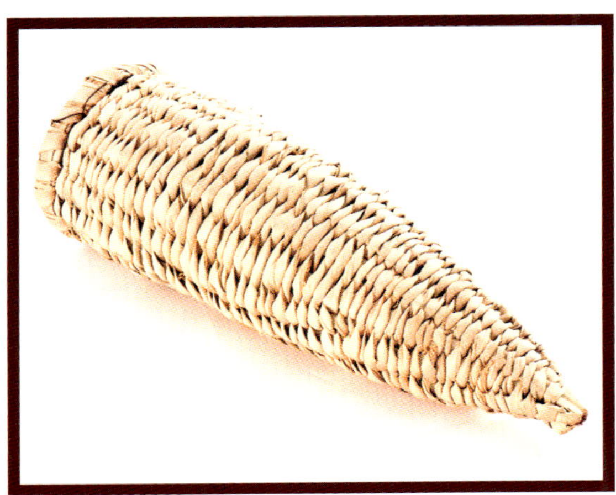

Before rubber became the standard material for condoms in the nineteenth century, cultures used various materials for protective barriers. They made condoms from goat's bladders, linen, silk, and palm leaves. Some African cultures even used woven reeds (*pictured*) as a form of contraception.

CHAPTER THREE

Female-Controlled Contraception

In 1914 US activist Margaret Sanger coined the term *birth control*. She wanted women to control their reproductive health without relying on men to decide for them. Sanger, originally a nurse, had left her career in 1912. She dedicated her life to promoting sex education and contraception. She wrote and published articles, pamphlets, and magazines about the topic.

Sanger's Crusade

In 1916 Sanger established the first US birth control clinic in New York City. In 1921 she founded the American Birth Control League, which later became Planned Parenthood. This is still one of the most prominent reproductive health-care providers in the US. Sanger was frequently harassed by law enforcement, arrested, and even jailed for her efforts. But she drew attention to the issue of contraception access, which soon gained mass public support. Sanger used legal appeals to challenge existing contraception laws. In 1936 Sanger convinced courts to reinterpret the Comstock Act. This change allowed physicians to distribute contraceptive

Sanger was the sixth out of eleven children. Sanger's mother also had seven miscarriages. Her mother died at the age of fifty due to health issues related to frequent pregnancies. Losing her mother so young motivated Sanger to advocate for women's reproductive rights.

materials and information to their patients. Later in her career, she traveled the world, promoting birth control in other countries including Japan and India.

A Surprising Ally

Sanger's fight for birth control coincided with the rise of the eugenics movement, which she supported. This movement advocated for selective breeding to create children with specific physical characteristics that the movement claimed would make a superior generation of humans. These characteristics were those of white, northern Europeans. Eugenics was a popular movement among US and Canadian scientists, physicians, and the general public in the 1920s and 1930s. Many eugenicists supported contraception and abortion, especially among the populations they deemed undesirable.

Eugenicists divided humans into two classes: fit and unfit. These divisions fell along racist and nativist lines, with "fit" people representing middle- and upper-class couples of northern European descent. "Unfit" people included Black and Indigenous people as well as immigrants from southern Europe and Ireland. The "unfit" group also included low-income and disabled individuals. In addition to encouraging these groups to use birth control, eugenicists often completed forced sterilization. This meant performing surgical procedures that would prevent "unfit" women from bearing children. The eugenics sterilization campaigns particularly targeted Indigenous women in the US and Canada.

The Mighty Pill

Since the earliest days of her fight for reproductive education, Sanger dreamed of a pill women could take to prevent pregnancy. In 1951 she approached scientist Gregory Pincus, who said such a pill might be possible. She helped fund his efforts to develop a hormonal birth control pill for women. Like many researchers of his time, Pincus relied on unethical methods to explore his theories about hormonal birth control. He experimented on women with mental disabilities without their consent before moving his tests to Puerto Rico, where contraceptive laws were less strict. There, Pincus ran clinical trials on low-income women with limited formal education. Many of these women were not aware they were involved in a test or told about the potential side effects of the pill.

Despite his questionable methods, Pincus's work was a success. In the 1960s the US Food and Drug Administration

Sterilizing Women

Throughout the 1900s eugenics beliefs in the US and Canada led to the forced sterilization of more than seventy thousand women. This practice overwhelmingly affected women of color and those with physical and mental disabilities. Between the 1930s and 1970s authorities forcibly sterilized one-third of women living in Puerto Rico, a US territory, in the name of population control. In the 1960s sterilization programs in North Carolina disproportionately targeted Black women. Between 1970 and 1976, 25 percent of Indigenous women living in the US were sterilized without their consent. The US government helped pay for many of these procedures.

An estimated twelve thousand Canadian First Nations women were forcibly sterilized between the 1970s and 2010s. In 2018 hundreds of Indigenous Canadian women sued their government for forced sterilizations occurring as late as 2017. In 2019 a Canadian doctor was convicted of forcibly sterilizing a First Nations woman.

The US also continued its forced sterilization practices well into the 2000s. In 2001, 148 female prison inmates in California were sterilized without their consent. California barred the practice in 2014, but it is still legal under a judge's order in thirty-one states. Some officials within the US criminal justice system offer convicted women shorter prison sentences or lesser fines if they agree to be sterilized.

Mary Franco was forcibly sterilized in 1934 at age thirteen under California's sterilization program.

approved the first hormonal birth control pill for widespread public use. The pill works by flooding the body with synthetic versions of the hormones estrogen and progesterone. These excess hormones prevent someone from ovulating, which means they are unable to get pregnant.

The Pill Takes Off

The pill was an instant success. By 1965 one out of every four married women under the age of forty-five had used it. Still, not everyone had equal access to the pill. Many states had laws banning contraceptive products, even among couples who were married. In 1970 the US government passed Title X. This law provided government funding for family planning and reproductive services across the country, increasing contraception access for low-income people. In 1972 the US Supreme Court struck down a Massachusetts law barring sales of contraception to unmarried people. This ruling meant everyone had legal access to contraception through their physicians. By this time, millions of people around the world were on the pill. And the pharmaceutical companies that manufactured the pill were making a lot of money.

Pill Pushback

Not everyone agreed the pill was a miracle drug. Many religious leaders came out against it, believing it conflicted with their religious teachings, particularly within the Catholic church. Some people and physicians also began to question if the pill was as safe as pharmaceutical companies had promised. In 1969 Barbara Seaman

REFLECT

How do cultural, religious, or personal beliefs shape attitudes toward the birth control pill?

The Marvelous Menstrual Cycle

Hormonal birth control alters the hormones involved in the menstrual cycle. This cycle lasts an average of twenty-eight days, although it can vary from person to person. Different hormone levels rise and fall during the cycle to prepare the body for conception and pregnancy. During the first part of the cycle, the body sheds the uterine lining. The lining exits the body in a flow of blood known as menstruation, which lasts several days. After menstruation, estrogen levels begin to rise. This thickens the uterine wall lining, preparing it for pregnancy, and triggers the body to ovulate—release an egg. Progesterone levels start rising during this time, which prepares the uterus to receive the egg. If a sperm successfully fertilizes the egg, the egg embeds itself in the uterine wall and grows into an embryo. If the egg is not fertilized, progesterone levels drop, triggering the egg and uterine lining to be released through menstruation, and the cycle starts again.

Most young women begin menstruating around the age of twelve, but it can start as young as seven. In the past, the average age was fourteen or older. Scientists aren't sure why people are having their first menstruation so early.

What about the Guys?

Women face much higher stakes with an unplanned pregnancy than their male partners. As a result, people have long considered birth control a woman's responsibility. Researchers have been working to develop male birth control pills since the 1970s. But male birth control pills are not yet available. The modern female birth control pill is safe and works well when taken correctly, but it's not 100 percent effective.

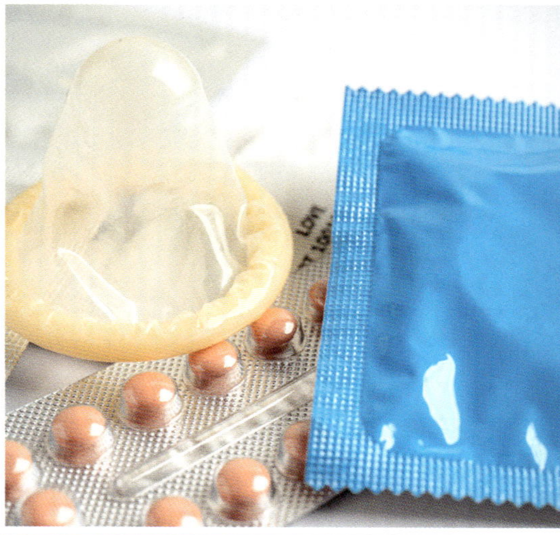

Approximately 750 million condoms are sold worldwide each year. The global condom market is expected to reach around $16.34 billion by 2029.

It's important for men to know their birth control options too. Condoms are one of the most effective forms of male birth control. When used correctly, they can prevent pregnancy 98 percent of the time and prevent STIs. When condoms are used along with female birth control pills, pregnancy is even less likely. There are various types of condoms available, including latex, polyurethane, and polyisoprene. Latex condoms are the most common, but alternatives are available for those with latex allergies.

Another birth control option for men is a vasectomy. This is a surgical procedure that prevents sperm from passing through the testicles. Although vasectomies are usually reversible, the procedure is best for people who are sure they don't want any more children.

published *The Doctor's Case Against the Pill.* The book contained testimonies of physicians and medical researchers who had observed troubling side effects associated with the pill, including a potential increased risk of cancer. Pharmaceutical companies did not warn people taking the pill about these side effects.

The Nelson Hearings

Seaman's book caught the attention of lawmakers. In 1970 US senator Gaylord Nelson held a series of congressional hearings on the dangers of the pill. During the hearings, lawmakers interviewed only male physicians and researchers. A group of women who had taken the pill and experienced side effects attended the hearing. These women were angry that lawmakers did not interview or consult with them during the hearings. They became furious as the hearings continued. They began to see birth control pills as a large-scale experiment pharmaceutical companies had been conducting on women without their consent. Some of the women shouted at the lawmakers, asking, "Why are you using women as guinea pigs?"

The hearings brought public attention to the dangers of the pill. Many people stopped taking it. The public response forced lawmakers and drug companies to take action. The US government passed laws requiring drug companies to disclose information about their drugs to consumers, including all potential side effects. Birth control manufacturers reduced the levels of hormones in the pill, making it much safer.

CHAPTER FOUR

Fighting for Reproductive Rights

While Sanger and reproductive rights groups were fighting to make contraception legal and more accessible, another fight was brewing over abortion rights. Starting in the 1850s many wealthy white people wanted smaller families with fewer children. Without reliable contraception methods, many people received abortions to achieve this goal. Meanwhile, immigrants and people of color were having many children. This concerned the AMA and many government leaders, who shared racist beliefs about eugenics, which were common at the time. The AMA took a strong stance against abortion and began working to ban the practice. Many of its physicians viewed banning abortion as a way to increase the white population and establish control over women's health care.

A Dangerous Practice

By 1910 medical education was firmly under the control of the AMA. Abortion was illegal in every state unless a physician determined it was necessary to save a pregnant person's life. However, these new laws didn't mean abortions never happened. People still sought abortions to end unwanted pregnancies. Thousands of immigrants and low-income people paid for dangerous abortions that untrained practitioners performed in unsafe conditions. Other people resorted to self-induced abortions, using unsafe methods and tools such as knitting needles to end their pregnancies. These illegal abortions led to thousands of hospitalizations and deaths each year.

Abortion was legal in Puerto Rico, and some US physicians performed illegal abortions there in secret. But such abortions were typically only accessible to wealthy white people who had the means to travel and pay for such services. Abortion laws were strict across North America. In 1931 the Mexican government passed a law imposing harsh penalties on abortions. Both abortion providers and their pregnant patients could face prison sentences of up to six years if found guilty of providing or receiving abortions. Canada also banned abortions in the early 1900s, but physicians who performed the procedure were rarely prosecuted.

By the 1950s people in the US were getting 1.2 million illegal abortions each year. Every year, up to ten thousand people died from complications related to illegal abortions. Activists established underground networks that provided safe, affordable, physician-performed abortions to people in need. While pregnant people were typically not criminally charged for seeking or getting abortions, those found guilty of aiding abortions faced losing their medical licenses, steep fines, and jail time. Some doctors who performed legal abortions to save someone's life faced criminal charges because courts later determined the procedure was unnecessary.

Changing Opinions

By the 1960s public views on abortion began to shift across North America, partly because of the large number of deaths caused by illegal abortions. Concern surrounding congenital disabilities also helped shift public perceptions of the practice. In the 1950s and early 1960s doctors commonly prescribed a drug called thalidomide to treat pregnancy symptoms, including nausea and insomnia. Canada and forty-six other countries approved the drug for pregnant people. It was not legal in the US due to concerns that it could cause congenital disabilities, but hundreds of US women purchased the drug in other countries, believing it was safe. However, doctors found that the medication caused severe congenital disabilities, including physical deformities and blindness. Many babies who had been exposed to thalidomide during pregnancy died within a few months after birth. Thalidomide affected more than ten thousand babies.

In 1962 a pregnant TV host from Arizona who had taken thalidomide traveled to Sweden to get an abortion after failing to get a legal abortion in the US. The media widely publicized the story, and one of the first-ever abortion polls found that more than half of Americans supported the woman's decision. Two years later, activists formed the first pro-abortion group aimed at changing US abortion law. Views in the medical establishment also became more open to the procedure. In 1966 nine California gynecologists faced a lawsuit after performing an abortion on a pregnant woman infected with rubella, a disease that often causes congenital disabilities. Physicians around the US came to the doctors' defense, including the leaders of more than one hundred medical schools.

Abortion in the Age of Genetic Testing

In modern times, pregnant people have access to detailed prenatal testing. This testing, typically performed in the first trimester, can alert parents and physicians to an increased risk of genetic disorders that will affect the child, as well as potential congenital disabilities, such as Down syndrome, heart defects, missing limbs, or blood disorders. The impacts of some of these disorders vary widely. Some are life-threatening, meaning the fetus will not survive the pregnancy or the child will die within two years. Children with other genetic disorders may live between thirty and fifty years with proper treatment. Other disorders may not affect the child's lifespan but may mean they will require many additional resources and support throughout their life.

Genetic testing can give future parents important information as they prepare for the birth of their child. But it can also leave parents with difficult decisions. Many parents choose to terminate their pregnancies when they learn there may be an issue with the fetus. This is a highly personal decision that is made between the pregnant person and their physician. However, critics have compared terminating pregnancies based on prenatal testing to eugenics, because it reduces the number of people with disabilities.

About 65 to 70 percent of pregnant individuals in the US undergo some form of genetic testing during their pregnancy.

Making Abortion Legal

By 1969 abortion was the most common form of birth control globally, with more than thirty million people terminating their pregnancies each year. That year Canada legalized abortion in some situations, such as when the pregnant person's health was at risk. Other countries loosened restrictions on the procedure as well. US states also took steps to legalize abortion. Colorado was the first state to modify restrictions on abortion laws in 1967. The legislation permitted abortion in cases of rape, incest, threats to the mental or physical health of the pregnant person, and congenital disabilities. California and North Carolina introduced similar reforms that same year. By 1969 six more states had less restrictive abortion laws, including Maryland and Oregon.

Roe v. Wade

As more states started rolling back abortion restrictions, US pro-abortion activists began looking for a way to change federal laws to guarantee the right to abortion in every state. In 1969 Norma McCorvey from Dallas, Texas, was denied an abortion for an unplanned pregnancy. At the same time, two pro-abortion lawyers, Sarah Weddington and Linda Coffee, were looking

Norma McCorvey (Jane Roe in *Roe v. Wade*) never had an abortion. By the time the US Supreme Court gave its decision, she had been forced to carry out her pregnancy, and her child was adopted.

for a case that would help them challenge the federal laws surrounding abortion. Weddington and Coffee approached McCorvey and agreed to represent her in a lawsuit against Dallas County's district attorney, Henry Wade. To protect McCorvey's identity, the lawyers gave her a pseudonym, Jane Roe.

The US Supreme Court heard *Roe v. Wade* in 1972. Weddington and Coffee argued that the US Constitution guaranteed a woman's right to have an abortion. On January 22, 1973, the court issued its opinion. While it didn't agree with Weddington and Coffee's belief that women were entitled to an abortion at any time and for any reason, it decided that the Fourteenth Amendment of the Constitution guaranteed a woman's right to abortion, with certain restrictions.

"No State shall make or enforce any law which shall abridge the privileges or immunities of citizens of the US; nor shall any State deprive any person of life, liberty, or property, without due process of law; nor deny to any person within its jurisdiction the equal protection of the laws."

—Fourteenth Amendment to the US Constitution

The *Roe v. Wade* ruling declared that women had a federal right to an abortion for any reason during the first trimester of pregnancy or before the fetus was viable—able to survive outside the womb. In the second trimester, after viability, individual states could not ban abortions entirely, but they could impose restrictions on the conditions under which an abortion could be performed. In the third trimester, state laws could prohibit abortions as long as the pregnant person's life or health were not at risk. Overnight, first-trimester abortions were legal in every state in the US.

When Does Life Begin?

When the Supreme Court was considering *Roe v. Wade*, the justices tried to balance a person's right to privacy with an unborn child's right to life. Scientists, religious leaders, and politicians still grapple with the issue of when life begins. Most pro-life supporters believe that life begins at conception, when a sperm fertilizes an egg. In their view, abortion is immoral and should be illegal at any stage of pregnancy because it's taking a life. Some scientists and doctors argue that life begins later, although they can't agree on when. Some think it is when the fetus reaches a certain week of pregnancy or level of development. Others believe life begins when the fetus can survive outside the womb.

To understand more about the different viewpoints on when life begins, it may help to know about the stages of pregnancy. The average pregnancy lasts about forty weeks, divided into three trimesters. Most people discover they are pregnant through a positive pregnancy test or a missed period in the first trimester, at around six weeks. The second trimester is from thirteen to twenty-eight weeks. During this time, the pregnant person will likely feel the fetus move. Each perspective on when life begins has its own reasons based on biology, technology, and personal beliefs.

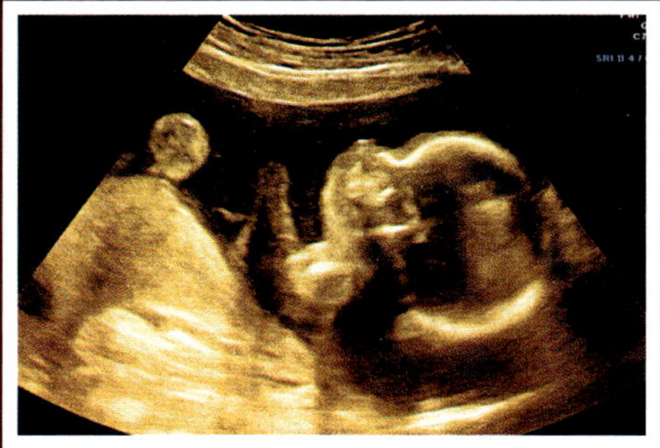

An ultrasound image of a fetus at twenty-four weeks. With modern medical advancements, babies born this early can now survive, whereas in 1973 a fetus only became viable during the third trimester.

A Post-*Roe* America

After the *Roe v. Wade* decision, abortion was more polarizing than ever before. Activists on both sides of the debate were divided into two main groups. Pro-life activists fought to overturn *Roe v. Wade* and replace it with a federal abortion ban. Pro-choice activists fought to increase abortion access and remove second and third trimester restrictions. The pro-life side of the debate earned a victory with the Hyde Amendment in 1976 when the US government banned the use of federal money to aid in abortions. This primarily affected low-income people who relied on government-funded programs to pay for their health care. The same year, the Republican Party officially added banning abortion to its party platform, firmly aligning itself with the pro-life movement. Democrats in turn adopted pro-choice values. Abortion was now not only a moral and medical issue, but a political one. Decisions made about abortion laws during this period continued to influence elections, legislation, and social attitudes for many years.

Pro-choice and pro-life protesters clash at the US Supreme Court Building in 2015.

CHAPTER FIVE

Rolling Back Rights

The Supreme Court rulings of the 1970s legalized contraception and abortion across the US. But they didn't guarantee all people equal access to abortion or contraception. State laws varied about abortions after the first trimester. And many low-income people and those living in rural areas lived in health-care deserts—areas where people need to travel thirty minutes or more to access health care. For people without reliable transportation, this could make it challenging or impossible to access a birth control prescription. These people had an even more difficult time accessing clinics that performed abortions. Additionally, health insurance companies often didn't cover birth control. Medicaid, the government health insurance program that many low-income people use, could not legally pay for contraception or abortions under US law. These barriers disproportionately affected people of color, who were much more likely to live in rural and economically disadvantaged parts of the country. Canadians also faced similar accessibility issues, with most abortion clinics centered in urban communities.

Abortion and Religion

Throughout the twentieth and twenty-first centuries, thoughts on abortion have been closely tied to religious views. Jewish law states that a fetus is not a person until birth, and the religion officially supports the practice of abortion. Islamic views vary, but most Islamic scholars believe abortion should be allowed in most circumstances until seventeen weeks.

In Christianity, abortion views vary by denomination. The Catholic, Baptist, and Evangelical churches take official stances against abortion. While a majority of Christians oppose abortion for moral reasons, they still support a woman's right to choose and believe abortion should be legal in most cases. People who consider themselves more religious and regularly attend church have a more extreme view of the issue. This group is more likely to believe abortion should be illegal in all circumstances. These religious divisions spill over into regional divides. Mexico legalized abortion in 2023. However, in a country where 80 percent of citizens identify as Catholic, there is still a cultural stigma around abortion. For example, people in Mexico who have abortions may find themselves socially isolated from religious friends and family members.

Activism

The pro-life movement also grew during the 1970s. Republicans played a key role in bringing Evangelical Christians into the pro-life effort, expanding its base beyond Catholic supporters. This also helped attract new, reliable

During the Summer of Mercy in 1991, police arrest and carry away a pro-life protester at an abortion clinic. Thousands of anti-abortion protesters blocked clinic entrances, staged sit-ins, and crowded the streets in Wichita, Kansas.

Republican voters. In 1980 Republican Ronald Reagan won the presidential election largely because of pro-life supporters. In the wake of *Roe v. Wade*, pro-life supporters held protests outside abortion clinics, often harassing the providers and their patients. They physically barred patients from accessing clinics, sometimes lying on the ground to block sidewalks. The activists argued with patients seeking abortions, trying to convince them to change their minds. In 1991 protesters staged a forty-two-day siege of abortion clinics in Wichita, which the pro-life movement called the Summer of Mercy. The siege included a rally featuring more than 25,000 protesters. More than 2,600 people were arrested during the Summer of Mercy.

Violence and Terror

Throughout the 1980s and 1990s an extremist wing of the pro-life movement resorted to violence and destruction to promote its cause. Between 1977 and 2023 pro-life extremists were responsible for eleven murders, forty-two bombings, and more than five hundred assaults. The extremists targeted abortion clinics, providers, patients, and volunteers. Pro-life extremists also burned down or destroyed abortion clinics. Similar acts of violence took place in Canada, where abortion was legalized in 1988. In 1992 pro-life extremists bombed a Toronto clinic. While many pro-life leaders condemned such acts of violence, others appeared to endorse them.

More than three hundred thousand people gathered in Washington, DC, for the Mobilize for Women's Lives pro-choice rally on November 12, 1989. This rally was one of more than one thousand abortion rights events happening that day in cities and towns across the US.

The pro-choice movement also engaged in activism but rarely resorted to violence. Pro-choice activists focused on expanding access to abortion clinics. Some volunteers formed networks to provide transportation and funding to people seeking abortions in states with less restrictive laws. Other volunteers offered support to people getting abortions, helping them walk past the pro-life protesters that had become a daily presence at many abortion clinics. Pro-choice activists also fought to improve accessibility to birth control, which would help reduce the number of abortions.

Political Action

While pro-life activists protested and rallied against abortion clinics, pro-life politicians worked to chip away at laws allowing abortion and contraception access in the US. Republican leaders began appointing pro-life judges to courts across the country. Eventually, some of these judges advanced to the US Supreme Court. In 1992 the Supreme Court's ruling in *Casey v. Planned Parenthood* upheld the right to abortion but allowed states to add more restrictions. These restrictions included requiring minors to get a parent's or guardian's permission, mandating that married women notify their husbands, and requiring clinics to provide information

Planned Parenthood is a major provider of sex education, reaching more than one million people annually through online resources, workshops, and school programs.

about alternatives to abortion, such as adoption. After receiving this information, a person had to wait twenty-four hours before a doctor could perform the abortion.

These restrictions particularly affected low-income people, who often lacked the resources to make multiple trips to an abortion provider. *Casey v. Planned Parenthood* also made abortions riskier and more expensive for many abortion clinics. As a result of the ruling, state laws surrounding abortion restrictions became less clear. Clinics risked lawsuits for performing abortions that unintentionally violated state law. Some states also passed new requirements for abortion providers, such as forcing them to convert abortion clinics into small hospitals or gain the ability to admit patients into local hospitals. These requirements were often expensive and sometimes impossible to fulfill. This put more pressure on abortion clinics, forcing some to close. In 1988 the US had 2,582 abortion providers. By 2000 that number had dropped to 1,819, with 87 percent of counties having no providers. The closures overwhelmingly affected rural counties.

In 2012 Texas passed a law requiring people seeking abortions to receive sonograms before the procedure and listen to the fetus's heartbeat. Other states passed similar laws. Many pro-choice supporters felt such laws were cruel to people already facing a difficult decision to end a pregnancy, particularly if the pregnancy was desired and the person was ending it due to health reasons. In addition, these restrictions added more time to

"What good is a law that adds only pain and difficulty to perhaps the most painful and difficult decision a woman can make? Shouldn't women have a right to protect themselves from strangers' opinions on their most personal matters?"

—Carolyn Jones, receiver of an abortion in Texas in 2012

the abortion process. This affected people who had to take time off work and travel to receive the procedure. As with other abortion restrictions, these disproportionately affected low-income people and people of color.

The closing of abortion clinics also reduced access to other reproductive health-care services. Planned Parenthood is one of the best-known abortion providers in the US. It primarily serves low-income and other disadvantaged patients. Abortions account for only 3 percent of Planned Parenthood's health services. It also offers STI screening and treatment, contraception, sexual education, cancer screening, and other preventative health care. As abortion laws forced Planned Parenthood clinics to close, people lost access to these health-care services too.

Two Steps Forward, One Step Back

While states continued passing new restrictions on abortion, another law improved birth control access for millions of people across the US. In 2010 US president Barack Obama signed the Patient Protection and Affordable Care Act (ACA). This law aimed to give all US citizens health insurance. States had to offer insurance plans to those who didn't have access to private insurance or qualify for Medicaid. The law required companies with fifty or more full-time workers to offer their employees insurance. The ACA also required all insurance companies to fully cover contraceptive and preventative reproductive care at no cost to the patient. In 2012 more than 63 million US women had access to affordable birth control, saving them more than $1 billion.

The victory for reproductive justice was short-lived. In 2012 two companies owned by Christian families sued the Obama administration, arguing that the ACA's new contraception law violated their right to religious freedom. One of the companies was Hobby Lobby. The Supreme Court heard the case *Burwell v. Hobby Lobby* in 2014. The court agreed with Hobby Lobby, with the five Republican-appointed justices outvoting the four Democrat-appointed ones. This court ruling meant that some businesses could refuse to include birth control in their employee health insurance plans if it went against their religious beliefs.

Many Republicans and religious leaders celebrated the Hobby Lobby victory, while others viewed it as a blow to reproductive rights. In 2016 Republican Donald Trump was elected president. During his term, he appointed three conservative justices to the Supreme Court, creating a stronger conservative majority and shifting the Court's balance of power. He chose the new justices from a list approved by pro-life supporters. For the first time, pro-life activists' biggest goal was now within reach—overturning *Roe v. Wade*.

The Road to *Dobbs*

In 2020 Trump lost re-election to Democrat Joe Biden. But the balance of power in the Supreme Court stayed the same. Pro-life activists had been waiting for the right case that might overturn *Roe v. Wade*. In 2021 they had a chance with *Dobbs v. Jackson Women's Health Organization*.

In 2018 Mississippi passed a law banning most abortions after fifteen weeks of pregnancy, and the Jackson Women's Health Organization sued the state. The case was named *Dobbs v. Jackson Women's Health Organization*, after Thomas Dobbs, the state health officer. The Jackson Women's Health Organization argued that the law violated *Roe v. Wade* because it banned abortions before the fetus would be viable.

The Supreme Court heard arguments in 2021. In 2022 the court released a decision that shocked reproductive rights advocates across the US. The six conservative justices ruled in favor of Dobbs, declaring that the constitutional right to privacy did not protect a woman's right to an abortion. With this ruling, the justices overturned *Roe v. Wade*.

After *Dobbs*

When the justices announced the *Dobbs v. Jackson Women's Health Organization* ruling, thirteen states had trigger bans in place to ban abortion. Trigger bans were laws already written and waiting to be enacted if *Roe v. Wade* was overturned. The strictest of these bans prohibited abortion after six weeks, before many people even know they are pregnant. Texas passed a law that lets private citizens sue anyone who helps someone travel to another state for an abortion. This means a person could be taken to court for driving someone to an out-of-state clinic or giving them money for the trip.

Some states still allowed abortions if the pregnant person's life was in danger. But only physicians could decide if this was true. If the doctor was sued and the court disagreed with the doctor's decision, the doctor could face fines and lose their medical license. Because of this, some physicians refused to treat pregnant people with complications until they were close to dying. Some emergency physicians in states with restrictive abortion laws refused to treat pregnant people at all, fearing they'd be sued.

REFLECT

What were the unintended implications of passing and then overturning *Roe v. Wade*? How did this affect US reproductive health care as a whole?

CHAPTER SIX

Hearing Her

In 2017 tennis star Serena Williams gave birth to her first child via cesarean section. Immediately after giving birth, Williams experienced leg numbness and extreme pain. When she told the medical staff at the hospital, they dismissed her symptoms. The next day, Williams had trouble breathing. She had experienced blood clots in her lungs in the past, and she suspected it was happening again.

Williams quickly alerted the nurse to the life-threatening condition. Williams was surprised when the nurse dismissed her symptoms again and said her pain medication

Serena Williams won her seventh Wimbledon singles title in 2016. In 2017 while two months pregnant, she claimed the Australian Open title.

was likely just making her confused. Eventually, Williams said to the nurse, "I'm telling you, this is what I need." This convinced the nurse to bring the physician in to examine her. The doctor soon realized Williams had multiple blood clots that needed to be surgically removed. After many surgeries and medications, Williams survived. But thousands of other people across the country aren't so lucky.

Health Gaps

The US has the highest mortality rate of pregnant people in high-income nations. This is the rate at which people die from complications related to pregnancy or childbirth. In 2023 the US mortality rate of pregnant people was 19 per 100,000 births. However, Black women faced a rate of 50 per 100,000, more than double that of white women. Indigenous women also had nearly twice the risk of white women.

"There's so much judgment. If you're too calm, then they say, 'Oh, you're not sick. You don't look sick.' And then if you're crying and moaning, they say you're exaggerating. I don't really know what they want from us . . ."

—Amy Mason-Cooley, a Black patient who has struggled to get treatment for a blood disorder

The reasons for this disparity are complicated, but some go back to racist beliefs dating back hundreds of years. Like Williams, many Black women report that their pain is dismissed or they are treated with bias by health-care providers. A 2016 study showed that almost half of medical students believe that Black people have thicker skin and experience less pain than white people. Because of these beliefs, many Black patients struggle to have their concerns taken seriously. False stereotypes about Black people's pain tolerance

The Hear Her Campaign

More than 80 percent of pregnancy deaths are preventable with proper intervention and health care. In 2020 the US Centers for Disease Control and Prevention (CDC) launched the Hear Her campaign to tackle this issue. The CDC's goal was to reduce the number of deaths and complications by raising awareness about pregnancy and postpartum issues and empowering people to speak up about their health concerns. The campaign encourages health professionals to take the concerns of their patients seriously.

> "A person knows their body best. Listening and acting upon their concerns during or after pregnancy could save a life."
>
> — Dr. Wanda Barfield, Director of the CDC's Division of Reproductive Health

Research into the effectiveness of the Hear Her campaign has shown that it has improved communication between pregnant and postpartum people and their health-care providers.

also make doctors less likely to prescribe pain medication. One study found that doctors were 22 percent less likely to prescribe pain medication to a Black patient than to a white patient.

Barriers to Care

Black patients are also disproportionately more likely to face barriers to health care than white patients. In the 2010s the US and Canada began facing a shortage of obstetrician-gynecologists (OB-GYNs). An OB-GYN is a medical doctor specializing in women's health before, during, and after pregnancy. In the US, nearly half of all counties don't have a single OB-GYN, meaning people must travel for their care. In 2022 more than 2.2 million women of childbearing age lived in a health-care desert. This issue disproportionately affects people of color and low-income people, who are also less likely to have health insurance.

Most pregnancy-related deaths happen in the postpartum period, which is the first few months after a baby is born. To help limit the number of deaths, the World Health Organization recommends people receive at least four postpartum check-ups within six weeks of giving birth to make sure they are healing properly. In the US, insurance companies sometimes cover one check-up, although state insurance programs such as Medicaid often don't cover any postpartum care. As a result, nearly half of postpartum people skip their postpartum checkups. Many low-income people are also not able to take the time they need to recover after giving birth. The US is one of only six countries that does not offer some form of paid maternity leave. Because of this, many people return to work too soon after giving birth.

Gender-Affirming Care

Gender-affirming care includes medical and psychological services that support a person's gender identity. It can include hormone therapy, surgeries, counseling, and social support to help individuals feel more comfortable in their gender. Gender-affirming care plans typically begin with low-risk changes, including counseling and altering how a person expresses their gender identity through clothing, hairstyles, and more. Patients may progress to medications, such as hormone therapy. While these medications can cause changes to a person's body, such as the growth of body hair or voice changes, the effects are reversible if the medicines are stopped. Some patients may eventually choose to undergo surgery to better align their anatomy with their gender identity. Doctors rarely perform surgeries on people under the age of eighteen. Choosing to undergo gender-affirming care is a big decision. Depending on the scope of the treatment, it can affect how a person is viewed socially. It can also permanently affect a person's fertility and other characteristics.

When some politicians speak about gender-affirming care, they often make it seem dangerous and harmful, especially for young people. Others who oppose gender-affirming care argue that it is too risky. However, studies show that quality gender-affirming care improves mental health in people who are transgender. Transgender youth are three times more likely to have suicidal thoughts than their cisgender peers. Young people who undergo gender-affirming care are 73 percent less likely to experience suicidal thoughts than their transgender peers who have not undergone treatment.

Gender-affirming care varies in North America. Canada provides it through public health care. In Mexico, gender identity recognition has improved, but access is limited outside major cities. In the US, some states restrict treatments, while others protect access.

Fighting for LGBTQ+ Care

The LGBTQ+ community also faces barriers to reproductive care. These barriers include stigma, discrimination, and state laws. Many LGBTQ+ patients say they have faced discrimination from doctors and hospitals. One in four transgender patients delays getting medical care due to concerns of potential discrimination.

Many transgender people report that their biggest barrier to care is lack of access. Transgender patients report issues in finding doctors and health-care providers with experience and expertise in providing gender-affirming care. Some doctors may not fully understand what transgender patients need or may ignore important health-care needs such as birth control, preventative health screenings, or sexual health information. State laws also affect the LGBTQ+ community's access to reproductive care. More than twenty states have passed laws limiting gender-affirming care for transgender people under the age of eighteen.

Discrimination in LGBTQ+ health care often involves bias, stigma, and unequal treatment. Many face refusal of care, especially in reproductive health services, due to their sexual orientation, gender identity, or intersex status.

REFLECT

How do your identity and background shape your views on reproductive health-care access and equity?

CHAPTER SEVEN

Talking about Sex Education

In 2022 Florida governor Ron DeSantis signed the Parental Rights in Education Bill into Florida state law. The new law barred teachers from teaching or discussing LGBTQ+ issues, including gender identity, or sexual education to elementary students. The law was part of an ongoing debate between conservatives and liberals over LGBTQ+ information in schools. Conservatives argued that parents, not teachers, had the right to expose their kids to LGBTQ+ topics at a time and place that aligned with their family's values. Liberals argued that laws including Florida's were discriminatory and severely limited young people's ability to learn about their bodies and health. Regardless of the law's intent, the vague wording made it nearly impossible for teachers and school districts to address any sort of LGBTQ+ information without risking a lawsuit against them.

The Knowledge Gap

The Parental Rights in Education Bill drew attention to one of the most significant disparities in reproductive health care facing young people—sex education. Sex education

A southern California high school teacher guides a discussion on sexual abstinence, emphasizing it as a method of preventing pregnancy and STIs.

covers reproductive health, STIs, gender identity, contraception, body image, consent, and much more. This information helps young people understand their bodies and take ownership of their health and wellness. But the US has no federal laws that determine whether or how educators should teach sex education. Instead, these decisions are left to individual states to decide. As a result, where a person lives and attends school is a huge factor in determining what kind of sex education they receive.

As of 2023, thirty US states and the District of Columbia require sex education in public schools. However, only eighteen of these states require the information to be medically and factually accurate. Seventeen states teach only abstinence, meaning students don't learn about sexual activity, contraception, or birth control. Twelve states require students to learn about consent during sex education. Only ten states require schools to present LGBTQ+ identities and gender-affirming care positively. And four states forbid teachers from discussing LGBTQ+ care or answering questions about it. Such policies are harmful to LGBTQ+ youth. Research has shown that LGBTQ+ youth are more likely to experience

Period Poverty

Period poverty describes some people's lack of access to both proper menstrual products and knowledge about how to use them. Over a lifetime, the average US woman will spend $6,000 on menstrual supplies. Although menstrual products, such as tampons, pads, and menstrual cups, are medically necessary, people must pay for them out of their own pockets. In 2022 twenty-two states had additional taxes on menstrual items as luxury products. The high price of these items can make it challenging for low-income people to afford them each month. One study found that two-thirds of low-income women said they struggled to afford menstrual care items. People who receive government assistance to purchase food have resorted to selling their food stamps to buy pads and tampons, which are not included in the federal food program. People who can't afford the necessary supplies may miss work or school during their periods. One study found that one in five young people who menstruate have missed school because they did not have access to menstrual products.

Many people experience stigma and shame around their periods. Such stigma might include stereotypes about how people might act while menstruating, negative jokes about periods, and general discomfort around menstruation. Such stigmas affect the quality of information young people receive about menstruation, particularly in states with limited sex education programs. However, some students are taking matters into their own hands. In 2024 a group of high school students in Minnesota convinced lawmakers to provide free period products to all students in school restrooms. Their success challenged the stigma around periods, encouraging open conversation and normalizing access to menstrual care in Minnesota schools.

mental health issues, including suicide attempts, than their straight, cisgender classmates. Providing an environment where LGBTQ+ students can feel safe learning about and expressing their identities has been shown to improve mental health outcomes.

Fighting Back

Many organizations have stepped up to fight for better access to reproductive health information for young people. Planned Parenthood has long fought for better sex education. The organization trains sex educators to teach age-appropriate sex education topics to all ages, with some programs especially tailored to the LGBTQ+ community. They offer free digital resources for young people who don't have access to accurate information in their public schools. Planned Parenthood also works with state and federal lawmakers to improve laws around sex education.

REFLECT

Do you think there should be federal laws determining how sex education is taught in schools? Why or why not?

The Sexuality Information and Education Council of the United States (SIECUS) is another organization that fights to make sex education more equitable across the US. In addition to publishing sex education resources, SIECUS works to change how sex education is taught in the US. The organization believes that quality sex education helps young people manage their health and improves their overall quality of life.

The Youth Pride Association (YPA) and the Trevor Project provide resources specifically to LGBTQ+ youth. YPA works to provide equitable access to information about LGBTQ+ health care in schools. It also works directly with educators to

US Sex Education Report Card

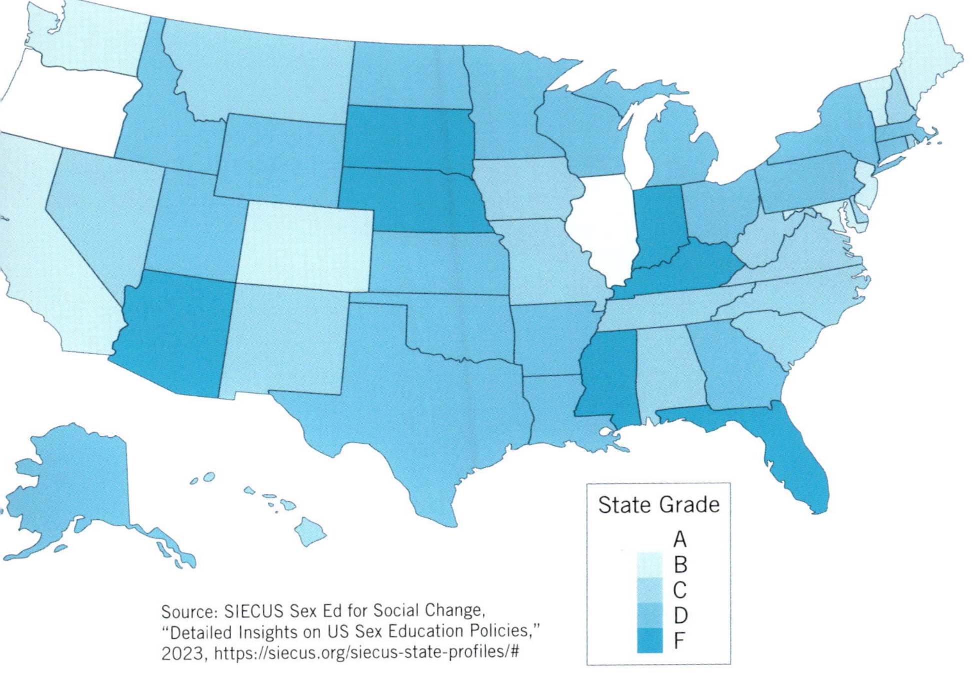

Source: SIECUS Sex Ed for Social Change, "Detailed Insights on US Sex Education Policies," 2023, https://siecus.org/siecus-state-profiles/#

In 2023 SIECUS graded each US state based on the quality of its sex education. Some of the criteria for grading states included medical accuracy, LGBTQ+ inclusivity, contraception instruction, and learning about healthy relationships.

turn schools into safe, inclusive spaces for LGBTQ+ students. The Trevor Project addresses mental health issues that many LGBTQ+ teens face. The group offers 24/7 free crisis counseling as well as resources to help LGBTQ+ youth discuss and understand their identities. The Trevor Project also works to pass laws to reduce discrimination against LGBTQ+ people and make their communities a safer place for them.

CONCLUSION

Taking Back Your Body

The fight for reproductive justice has had many ups and downs. Despite recent restrictions on abortion access, gender-affirming care, and sex education, most people in North America support improving reproductive rights. Sixty-three percent of Americans believe abortion should be legal in most or all cases. Following the *Dobbs v. Jackson Women's Health Organization* ruling, voters in several states, including Kansas, Kentucky, and Ohio, voted to protect abortion rights in their state constitutions. In Canada, 80 percent of people support abortion rights. And in Mexico, almost 50 percent of citizens support abortion rights despite high rates of social, cultural, and religious stigma.

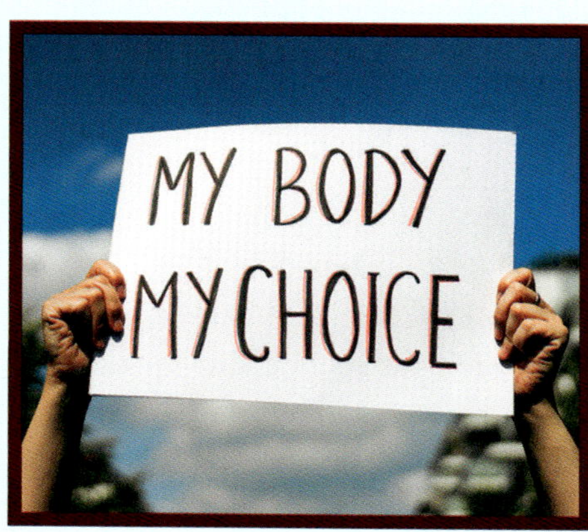

Many people who are pro-choice use the slogan "my body, my choice" to describe their beliefs.

In the US, the debate over reproductive rights remains unresolved, and legal and political battles over access to gender-affirming care, abortion, and contraception are ongoing. But organizations around the country are working to protect reproductive rights.

Take Control

Regardless of your sex or gender identity, you can join the reproductive rights movement by taking control of your reproductive health.

- Get educated. Take the time to learn about your body. If your school doesn't offer a fact-based sex education program, seek reliable information online. Or become an advocate for sex education at your school!
- Be an ally. Support the reproductive rights of people outside your personal experience. You don't need to be a member of the LGBTQ+ community to stand up for equitable LGBTQ+ health care. You don't need to be able to get pregnant to support people fighting for access to birth control and safe, legal abortion.
- End the stigma surrounding reproductive health issues by talking openly about periods, consent, contraception, and other related issues.
- Recognize discrimination and bias in health care and throughout your community. Call it out when you see it.
- Know your body. You are the expert of your own body. If something feels wrong, speak up and insist on getting the care you need.
- You have a right to reproductive health care. You have autonomy over your own body, and you get to decide what happens to it. The choice is yours.

GLOSSARY

abortion: the act of intentionally ending a pregnancy

abstinence: to willingly restrain oneself from sexual activity

anesthesia: a procedure used to prevent patients from feeling pain during surgeries or medical treatments

autonomy: the ability to make one's own decisions rather than being directed by someone else

bias: the realized or unrealized perception of a person or group of people that is not based on facts

cesarean section: a surgical procedure in which a baby is removed through an opening in the abdomen

congenital disability: a health condition or physical abnormality that a person is born with

consensual: done with the willingness of all parties involved

contraception: artificial methods used to prevent pregnancy. Spermicides (chemicals that stop sperm from reaching an egg), condoms, and birth control pills are all forms of contraception.

discrimination: unjust treatment of people or groups of people based on certain characteristics, such as race or gender

extremist: a person who has very strong, intense beliefs and is willing to go to extreme lengths to support those beliefs, often without considering the harm it might cause others. Extremists reject other people's ideas and may use violence to get their point across, believing their way is the only one.

fetus: a developing baby from eight weeks after conception to birth

gender dysphoria: distress caused by feeling that one's gender identity does not match the sex they were assigned at birth

gynecology: a branch of medicine associated with female anatomy, particularly the female reproductive system. A doctor who practices gynecology is often known as an OB-GYN.

incest: sexual activity between two people who are closely related to one another, such as parents and children or siblings

insomnia: a disorder that makes it difficult to fall asleep or stay asleep

LGBTQ+: stands for lesbian, gay, bisexual, transgender, and queer or questioning, with the plus (+) sign representing other sexual orientations, gender identities, and expressions that are not specifically covered by the acronym, such as asexual, intersex, pansexual, and others. It is an inclusive acronym describing people whose sexual and romantic orientations and gender identities are diverse and varied.

lobby: to influence the decisions of government officials or lawmakers, often by meeting with them

maternity leave: a period of time a pregnant person takes off from work after giving birth to care for their newborn baby

Medicaid: a US government program that helps cover medical expenses for low-income individuals and families

midwife: a person, usually a woman, trained to assist in childbirth

miscarriage: a spontaneous loss of pregnancy before twenty weeks of pregnancy, usually due to issues with the fetus

obstetrician: a doctor who specializes in pregnancy, childbirth, and the care of a pregnant person during and after pregnancy. They help with delivering babies and managing any complications that may arise during pregnancy or childbirth. They are often known as an OB-GYN.

ovulate: to release an ovum, or egg, for fertilization during the menstrual cycle

rape: sexual activity carried out against another person without their consent

sonogram: a visual image produced using ultrasound technology that can show a developing fetus

standardize: to make things the same by following specific rules or guidelines

sterilize: to permanently make a person unable to reproduce

stigma: a set of negative or unfair beliefs that a society or a group of people have about something

SOURCE NOTES

10 "wandering throughout the body": Elinor Cleghorn, *Unwell Women: Misdiagnosis and Myth in a Man-Made World* (New York: Dutton, 2021), 22.

10 "turn'd outside in.": Cleghorn, 2.

14 "In sorrow, thou . . . rule over thee.": Genesis 3:16, Twenty-First Century King James Bible, accessed August 2, 2024, https://www.biblegateway.com/passage/?search=Genesis%20 3:15-17&version=KJ21.

15 "obscene literature and . . . of immoral use.": "Comstock Act," Encyclopedia Britannica, accessed August 2, 2024, https://www.britannica.com/event/Comstock-Act.

25 "Why are you . . . as guinea pigs?": "Senate Hearings on the Pill," PBS: The American Experience, accessed August 1, 2024, https://www.pbs.org/wgbh/americanexperience/features/pill -senate-holds-hearings-pill-1970/.

31 "No State shall . . . of the laws.": "Fourteenth Amendment to the US Constitution, Section 1 Rights," Constitution Annotated, accessed August 1, 2024, https://constitution.congress .gov/browse/amendment-14/.

39 "What good is . . . most personal matters?": Carolyn Jones, "'We have no choice': One Woman's Ordeal with Texas' New Sonogram Law," *Texas Observer*, March 15, 2012, https://www .texasobserver.org/we-have-no-choice-one-womans-ordeal-with -texas-new-sonogram-law/.

44 "I'm telling you . . . what I need.": Alex Portée, "Serena Williams on her near-death experience after giving birth: 'No one was really listening,'" Today, updated August 9, 2022, https://www .today.com/health/womens-health/serena-williamss-essay-black -pregnancy-rcna23328.

44 "There's so much . . . want from us . . . ": Vidya Rao, "'You Are Not Listening to Me': Black Women on Pain and Implicit Bias in Medicine," Today, July 27, 2020, https://www.today.com/health /implicit-bias-medicine-how-it-hurts-black-women-t187866.

45 "A person knows . . . save a life.": "Hear Her Campaign: An Overview," CDC, May 15, 2024, https://www.cdc.gov/hearher /about/index.html.

SELECTED BIBLIOGRAPHY

"A Brief History of Birth Control." Our Bodies Ourselves Today at Suffolk University. Accessed August 1, 2024. https://www.ourbodies ourselves.org/health-info/a-brief-history-of-birth-control/.

Blakemore, Erin. "How US Abortion Laws Went from Nonexistent to Acrimonious." National Geographic, April 11, 2023. https://www .nationalgeographic.com/history/article/the-complex-early-history -of-abortion-in-the-united-states.

Cleghorn, Elinor. *Unwell Women: Misdiagnosis and Myth in a Man-Made World*. New York: Dutton, 2021.

Kolbert, Kathryn, and Julie F. Kay. *Controlling Women: What We Must Do Now to Save Reproductive Freedom*. New York: Hachette, 2021.

Littlejohn, Krystale E. *Just Get On the Pill: The Uneven Burden of Reproductive Politics*. Oakland, CA: University of California Press, 2021.

McKoy, Jillian. "Racism, Sexism, and the Crisis of Black Women's Health." The Brink: Pioneering Research from Boston University, October 31, 2023. https://www.bu.edu/articles/2023/racism-sexism -and-the-crisis-of-black-womens-health/.

Wade, Sabia. *Birthing Liberation: How Reproductive Justice Can Set Us Free*. Chicago: Chicago Review Press, 2023.

FURTHER INFORMATION

Books

Blumenthal, Karen. *Jane Against the World: Roe v. Wade and the Fight for Reproductive Rights*. New York: Roaring Brook Press, 2020.
Learn about the history of abortion in the United States and how it led to the landmark Supreme Court case *Roe v. Wade*.

Ford, Jeanne Marie. *Understanding Reproductive Health*. Minneapolis: Essential Library, 2021.
This title explores the ins and outs of reproductive health and teaches how to advocate for yourself in the doctor's office.

Nnachi, Ngeri. *Fighting for Reproductive Justice: Black Women Leading a Movement*. Minneapolis: Lerner Publications, 2024.
Learn about the history of reproductive rights in the US and meet some of the Black women fighting for equity in reproductive health care.

Starbuck Gerson, Emily. *From Silence to Solidarity: The Fight for LGBTQ+ Rights*. Minneapolis: Twenty-First Century Books, 2025.
This book explores the history of the LGBTQ+ community and its fight for rights in North America.

Yancey, Diane, and Tabitha Moriarty. *Beyond Sex Ed: Understanding Sexually Transmitted Infections*. Minneapolis: Twenty-First Century Books, 2024.
Learn everything you need to know about recognizing the symptoms, preventing, and talking about STIs as well as the history of discrimination faced by those who have experienced STIs.

Websites

5 Queer Sex Ed Resources by and for Young People
https://www.healthyteennetwork.org/news/queer-sex-ed-resources-young-people/
This website links to various resources to help young people who want to learn more about issues facing the LGBTQ+ community.

Health Care Equity
https://www.plannedparenthoodaction.org/issues/health-care-equity
Learn about some of the issues to health-care access facing people across the US.

Period Poverty: The Public Health Crisis We Don't Talk About
https://policylab.chop.edu/blog/period-poverty-public-health-crisis-we-dont-talk-about
This article explores the issue of period poverty and how it impacts people across the US.

State Profiles
https://siecus.org/siecus-state-profiles/
Find out how your state ranks in sex education policies using this helpful map provided by SIECUS.

What Is Gender-Affirming Care? Your Questions Answered
https://www.aamc.org/news/what-gender-affirming-care-your-questions-answered
This website explores the different types of gender-affirming care offered to people who have gender dysphoria.

INDEX

ABOUT THE AUTHOR

Lauren Kukla is an author, illustrator, and poet based in Minnesota. She has written more than one hundred books for kids of all ages. In her spare time, she loves gardening, Nordic skiing, and running. Lauren lives in a farmhouse on the edge of the woods with her husband, three kids, a dog, and a flock of chickens.

PHOTO ACKNOWLEDGMENTS

The images in this book are used with the permission of: © FatCamera/iStockphoto, pp. 5, 45; © U.S. Mission Geneva/Eric Bridiers/Wikimedia Commons, p. 7; © Rueff, Jakob/Wikimedia Commons, p. 9; © Ansel Adams/U.S. National Archives and Records Administration/Wikimedia Commons, p. 11; © imageBROKER.com GmbH & Co. KG/Alamy Photo, p. 17; © Library of Congress; P&P, p. 19; © Jae C. Hong/AP Images, p. 21; © vgajic/iStockphoto, p. 23; © sasirin pamai/iStockphoto, p. 24; © Cavan Images/iStockphoto, p. 29; © Bob Daemmrich/Alamy Photo, p. 30; © PEDRE/iStockphoto, p. 32; © DJMcCoy/iStockphoto, p. 33; © Associated Press/AP Images, p. 36; © mark reinstein/Alamy Photo, p. 37; © Sundry Photography/iStockphoto, p. 38; © Ian Rutherford/Alamy Photo, p. 43; © Renata Angerami/iStockphoto, p. 48; © Marmaduke St. John/Alamy Photo, p. 50; © Giraphics/Shutterstock Images, p. 53; © Amparo Garcia/iStockphoto, p. 54.

Cover Photo: © Jomkwan/iStockphoto

Design Elements: © Ezhevika/Shutterstock Images